FLOWER IN YOUR PAIN

When life throws you a curved ball, let it bend you towards another direction and then begin again.

Insights gained from life's unexpected occurrences.

Dionne-Sheree Smith

FLOWER IN YOUR PAIN
Author: Dionne-Sheree Smith
deesheree4@gmail.com
www.facebook.com/flowerinyourpain
Twitter: Dee@deesheree2
Copyright © 2014 by Dionne-Sheree Smith

DEDICATION

Many thanks go to God, my eternal strength and helper, my father and sister who formed a support structure of encouragement and to my mother, who in life, exemplified the true essence of a strong and resilient woman, and in death, displayed courage and faithfulness to God. Thanks also to my friends; Marcia, Latoya, Alece, Karlene, Belinda, James, Mark and Jamar who actively shared their thoughts with me while we discussed at length many of the topics mentioned in this book. Special thanks also to my other friends who chose to remain nameless, who took the time to read and offer their suggestions to make this book better.

I thank God especially for my children, Dominick and Deidre-Kay, my gifts from God, who each day remind me of the need to lead by example and to be what God has designed me to be.

CONTENTS

INTRODUCTION

I have always known that there were some things that I wanted to share and knew that my reason for sharing was mainly to touch lives. My life to date has been filled with some significant events that have caused me to pause, ponder and sometimes be perplexed. Through each event I have experienced some hurt, pain, embarrassment, but most of all, growth, because with every curved ball that was thrown, I gained some insights that proved crucial to my personal development. I have made mistakes and, no doubt, may make many more before I die, but I have found that life is not about regrets, it's about making the most out of what you have.

In this book you will find short stories re-telling some of my experiences; some funny while others are a bit more contemplative. Some are more insights than stories, but every reflection was as a result of personal growth. Additionally, I have shared some helpful tips that had helped me gain a deeper understanding of relationships with the aim of helping you.

As you read, you will find that this book is not one of straightforward instruction indicating how to actually achieve growth from unexpected circumstances, but rather looks at how to do this from a personal viewpoint. My stories and thoughts will show how I grew from my experiences and hopefully give you the inspiration to discover how to grow from your own situations. It is my hope that when you have come to the end of this reflective literary journey, you would have been encouraged, inspired and urged to become a better person and more importantly, the person that God has purposed you to be.

I am not a relationship advisor, marriage counselor or expert on any of the topics I have touched, neither am I pretending to be. I would also rather not be in the precarious situation of someone banging on my door stating that their partner told them that I gave them relationship advice or instructions that ended up in a broken relationship. Like you, I am still learning, but my aim is to share these insights and personal thoughts to help you in your journey to unearth your talents, to flower in your pain and to re-ignite your hope in life and your dreams. As you continue moving toward achieving your God-given purpose, here is my offering to you.

CHAPTER 1
SUDDENLY ALONE

Life has a funny way of throwing or should I say flinging things at you at varying speeds which sometimes catch you off guard. One minute you are experiencing a fulfilling, successful life, the other minute, the world seems to be falling apart.

Several years ago, I found myself in a situation that was quite similar to what people would describe as the perfect reason for a major meltdown. I was alone with two young children, earning a woefully insufficient salary in light of my expenses, facing an enormous mortgage and other financial issues while experiencing an emotional rollercoaster within.

Life, up to that point, was good albeit, with some ups and downs that caused some stirring along the way. Generally though, life was still okay. My children were born a couple years prior and were still very much reliant on their parents for their happiness. Indeed we never neglected to show them how much we loved them and always tried to spend as much time as we could with them.

I remember it well, that evening when the phone rang and suddenly things changed. "Dionne, he can't come home tonight." That call represented the crack in the walls that had secured me all those years. It also signaled the beginning of approximately two years of aloneness that tested all the strength in my being.

Every day was a challenge. First, not having him near was painful. Secondly, the financial burdens seemed insurmountable and although he offered some possible solutions, I was immobilized with fear to try. I would have gone under if it were not for faithful family members and friends who stood by us. I learnt how to prioritize and I soon understood the valuable lesson of sacrifice during those years.

I remember one fateful night when I was travelling home with my children and the fan belt in my car decided that that would the best time to burst. I was ready to walk the rest of the way with them even though I was not so sure how I would have managed to carry two children when they became tired. Just then, a stranger drove up and offered us a ride. Now my "mama didn't raise no fool" and I would not have accepted the offer under normal circumstances, but I prayed and decided to accept the provision that God had made. We reached home safely.

Thinking about that time still amazes me how provisions were made. I had insufficient disposable income. Now picture having to handle regular home expenses, car issues, school costs, mortgage, work issues, hurricane damages (yes even in the midst of all of that a hurricane had damaged the house), and then picture God stepping in every time. He sent angels in the form of persons who worked on the repairs, who were okay with being paid over time or not at all. He provided family and friends who gave money freely, friends who bought my children's school books, a school administration who drastically extended discounts on my children's school fees, a boss who was lenient in giving me time off from work and a friend who fixed the hurricane damages with no request for up- front payment. In the midst of that I had to even sell the only car I had and God provided a car that I could drive, and all I had to do was maintain it.

The lessons were clear to me then and still are. These I now share:

1) God will never give you more than you can handle. Now I have heard this statement many times and have believed it. From time to time however, I have caught myself marveling at someone else's circumstance and stating my belief that I could never undergo what they underwent. In fact many persons have said the same thing in reference to my experiences. I thought about it and have come to the conclusion that no one really knows how much they can bear until they are tested and are required to go through it. Only God knows the strength he has placed within you to endure. He is the only one who knows what you can bear. So, I have learnt that whatever the circumstance, if He has taken me to it, it is because He knows that I can go through it. He is not setting me up to fail but rather to be strengthened in Him.

2) Life is unpredictable. We are only asked to trust the Omniscient One and believe that all things are working together for our good. No man is an island. Even in the separation from a loved one, God provided a support system to undergird me when I felt all alone.

Isaiah 43:2
"When you pass through the waters, I will be with you; and when you pass through the rivers, they will not sweep over you. When you walk through the fire, you will not be burned; the flames will not set you ablaze".

New International Version (NIV)

3

CHAPTER 2
THE D-WORD

If someone were to tell me that after 14 years of marriage I would end up divorced, I would have replied in my best Mr. Brown's voice "the devil is a liar!" Tyler Perry's television character 'Mr. Brown' is the only character that stirs within me the best comedic response similar to what I would have said back then. Up until adulthood, the d-word wasn't in my vocabulary. In fact before entering marriage, it definitely wasn't in my thoughts. This had largely to do with my Christian upbringing and my own personal values on matrimony. All my life, I had never been taught to contemplate, or deal with matters concerning divorce. It was considered taboo, an unspoken tragedy that occurred but was hardly used in a Christian's vernacular. Even while it unfolded in my own life from decisions made, I, for a while, could not even say the word out loud and thus resigned myself to using the moniker, the "d-word" for mental ease.

The process was difficult and, through it all, I was disappointed at the overwhelming silence I heard from the church I was attending. You see, my experience was very public, where most persons were aware of what was taking place, but no one said a word. The leaders for the most part, preferred not to get involved. I understand now that their intervention would have had to be handled carefully because any action on their part could possibly have been resented. While going through it though, I felt the church had let me down. From the experience I have realized then and even now that in some churches, there is no strategy in place for handling matters of the heart. As a result, the hearts of the people bow to the pressure of pain and brokenness as they try to make sense of the chaos around them in solitude.

I however, acknowledge my close friends who were there for me during the pain. I was very much aware however, that most of them took my side, and I realized that, while they meant well, it wasn't very helpful to me because I needed to learn how to bear fruit from my pain. A one-sided view would not have helped me achieve that and neither would me playing the blame game.

Then there were those who constantly thanked God publicly for their wonderful marriages of however many years. "God has been good to me saints, very good! I thank God for my beautiful wife of 18 years, the wife who tends to my every need, who has been faithful to me, who still remains the only one for me." Now there may be some exaggeration in this report but I remember how badly I felt as I sat in the pew. I thought "hmmm so where does that leave me and all the others in my position?" Of course I knew that nothing was wrong with thanking God for a beautiful marriage, but I became sensitive to the level of frequency that this was done.

My church and social life were eventually affected because I felt the need to retreat from the gossip that was swirling about and from the conception that I was a failure in comparison to all the apparently successful married couples. I also felt quite early that I had no longer fitted in with the married folk, since most of the friends I had then were married. It was extremely uncomfortable to be around them. Some tried to include me, which was comforting, but it was still unsettling to be invited to birthday parties and, while my children were having fun, there I was looking around and noticing that I was the only Mom there, when everyone else had their partners with them. Some would say it was all in the mind and that I was the cause of some of the pain I felt. At one point I asked myself "where do I fit in? Where do I turn?"

This led me on a personal search for the deeper understanding of this experience. These I now share with you:

1) Mutual commitment is crucial. Whether you are a Christian or not, divorce is a reality and it takes just one partner to entertain the thought for it to become real in your life. One partner choosing to decide that she or he is throwing in the towel, one partner to decide that the grass is greener on the other side, one partner to decide that they want out and then the unthinkable happens. For, even though you may pray for God to change things around, if one partner has made their decision to go and has determined in their minds to stop trying, the mutual commitment that is necessary to keep the marriage afloat is now missing, and the fight to keep the marriage intact becomes a difficult, uphill task. The implication is not that God's power has weakened and that He is unable to change the situation, it rather shows the evidence of free will in action. Choice is a precious gift. What we choose to do with it is up to us. If an individual chooses to walk out of their marriage, that is their choice. The Jamaican saying goes "one hand caan clap", (meaning it takes two hands to clap). One person cannot save a marriage; it takes the commitment of two to continually work at it to achieve relationship success.

2) Never say never because this also can happen to you. Once humans are involved, it can. This is because humans are weak and fallible at times and they can respond to the temptation of being selfish, lustful or vindictive. The fact that one has to rely and trust another human being makes relationships so uncertain. Therefore my suggestion is never to judge others who are in this position, just continue to work hard on your own.

3) The d-word is what it is …divorce. It is something that no-one wants to experience or wish for anyone. If, for some reason, you find yourself in such a situation, seek help from those equipped to help, for I have found that, no matter how painful it is, it is not the end of the world, and it too shall pass.

4) Don't expect too much from your congregation. The church is really a group of people who are going through their situations just like you, who remind each other of God's faithfulness, and encourage each other to continue on in the faith. Expecting your leaders to always be there to tend to the emotional needs of each member is not only unrealistic but physically impossible. Additionally, not all leaders are equipped to really help and, in sensitive cases such as this, professional help would be best. I believe though that a ministry or programme should be developed in churches to first support married people who are struggling, to arrest the incidence of divorce. This support can be in the form of mentors, small groups or external counselors. Also, the church ought to provide a space for the grief of divorce and help restore divorced members to wholeness. This is an ideal opportunity to reach out to the brokenhearted and encourage these people who believe they have

failed. The fact is, most church members don't really know how to treat their friends who went through a divorce. They feel constrained to take sides and, to prevent all that, they eventually avoid their company altogether. No longer do they invite them to parties or other gatherings because they believe it would be awkward. The truth is, this assumption creates a sense of alienation and does more damage than good.

5) Divorce should be avoided at all cost. God hates divorce and expects us to fight for our marriages. My main point here is that even though your partner has chosen to stop trying, there is still a possibility that your relationship can be saved. It is true that with time, things can turn around. Waiting in this instance, would be a test of endurance and faith. Over time, the true desires of your partner will become clear and this will help guide the choices you both make towards each other and towards your marriage.

6) Divorce is damaging but you're not damaged goods. Contrary to popular belief, you are still the same person you were before the event, only this time recovering from hurt and pain. This recovery process does take time and people may classify you as "damaged" in their eyes. It does take a lot to overcome that mental hurdle, but it's not insurmountable. Surround yourself with trusted friends, the word of God and family, and you'll get through this, trust me you will. In fact, you will eventually get to a point where you would have discovered that you are stronger than you thought and that you have risen to a position of strength where you now have the ability to help others in similar situations. Additionally, you will get to a position where you realize that you still have a whole

lot to offer, and that others see in you things far deeper than you see. I know it's hard, but God believes in you and He is depending on you to fulfill the purpose that He has designed for you, whether you are divorced or not. Divorce is not the end, for there is still a purpose for you to fulfill. In many instances, divorce creates new beginnings. Just remember though that a successful new beginning will be determined by how well you learnt the lessons coming out of the experience.

Through the process, I uncovered some other insights that could mitigate against the possibility of experiencing this pain. Here's some food for thought:

1) Before marriage, talk about the issue of divorce and see how each of you responds to this subject. Ideally, there should be a resolve between both of you to never entertain the thought and that both of you will always commit to fighting for your marriage.
2) There should be a mutual agreement to achieve unbridled trust and to understand that achieving this helps to facilitate a greater level of communication in the relationship.
3) Believing that your marriage will succeed is a self-fulfilling prophecy. If you believe the best, you will do your best and refuse to give up even when things get hard. Giving up should not be an option.

1 Corinthians 13: 7
"It (love) always protects, always trusts, always hopes, always perseveres.

New International Version. (NIV)

Although you cannot control what your spouse says or does, if both of you personally shut the door on the divorce possibility, you're much more likely to succeed. If both of you want it bad enough, success in marriage can be yours.

CHAPTER 3
TO LOVE OR NOT TO LOVE

So I'm sitting here thinking, "Ok so my marriage is over… hmmm don't think I'll be going down that road again!" I actually start laughing, but then I stop and begin to wonder.

I've often travelled the journey in my mind many times. From teenage years, to young adulthood, to marriage, to present, and I have contemplated many of the concepts that had directed my choices then, some of which were admittedly misguided. For starters, as child, I, like many of the young girls then, was into the happily ever after notion, having grown up on fairy tales. I always had in the back of my mind that one day I would meet the man of my dreams and he would take me from my parents' home and forever take care of me, "O-K, then!". I now chuckle at the thought of my childhood naiveté.

By the time I was a young adult, I was mentally conditioned that I would find my husband in the church I had attended. It was natural. I was also conditioned to expect this husband to always want to be by my side and to naturally always be in love with me…forgive me, I paused for a moment trying to regain my composure from falling over laughing while re-reading this sentence. My goodness I was young!

I was also in a church era where an early marriage was a regular thing. I got married a couple months shy of my 22nd birthday and felt that I was ready. Now I am not about to say that that was a big mistake, but I will say that marrying young is tricky. At that age, in most cases, you haven't quite worked out what it is you want and also what is good for you. My advice to any young woman is to wait a while. Learn about yourself first. Find out what you like, what you don't like, your emotional needs, spiritual needs, communication style, plans for the future and your love languages. These love languages were introduced by author Dr. Gary Chapman, who wrote that individuals respond to love through different instigators, such as; words of affirmation, acts of service, receiving gifts, quality time or physical touch. I didn't have the answers to some of these areas in my life. I had to learn along the way, which was hard.

Here are some other things I learned in the process:
1) Marriage is not a solution for loneliness. Get a life! Loneliness comes with vulnerability. Also, it creates an imbalance in the relationship where one spouse relies on the other to fulfill their feelings of being lonely. She becomes clingy and dependent and almost incapacitated to live a complete life without her spouse being near. Good grief! This will lead to a dysfunctional relationship as there will always be times when one desires some "me" time. Ideally, if both partners learn to have separate pursuits and projects, then the coming together would be something to look forward to.
2) Marriage is not all about sex but it is a crucial ingredient for its success. Chemistry must be there. God made us with the ability to feel a physical connection with someone. Sexual desires are natural and must be regularly facilitated in a healthy relationship. Before you commit, set aside time for frank discussions on this topic and try to be as honest as possible about your physical desires and needs. Be honest with yourself. If the man doesn't cause your heart to do even a little

somersault when he walks in the room then, ahem, the chemistry between you may create a bomb rather than fireworks. Be mindful though, that the cardio cartwheels that I refer to are not necessarily triggered by his physical appearance but should also be triggered by the way he treats you and his character traits.

3) Marriage is not about receiving but rather, being prepared to give oneself unselfishly. Both individuals have to work hard at giving themselves to each other. Now this is an extremely vulnerable place to be because trusting your heart to someone is not very easy. I have learned from older couples that this takes time but it is quite possible. Truth is, in order for affection and love to naturally ooze out of a person towards another, both individuals must be committed to give themselves completely.

4) Marriage is not about the wedding ceremony or how grand it is. Rather, it is about the quality of life that two persons commit to creating when the splendour of the day has died down.

5) Marriage should not be a way of escape from your parents. For those of you who may be thinking that you have the most controlling parents in the world and think that the only way to escape is to marry early, think again, that's a recipe for disaster.

Some may say, I've loved and lost and many have said that if they were in my situation they would be afraid to love again. I really don't see it that way. I see it as a learning experience and a chance for me to grow.

A friend of mine, James, shared with me some of his thoughts while we were exploring this topic one day. We looked at questions such as; "Can one find true love after heartbreak? Can a heart that has been broken be mended to find love again, to express love, to receive love?" We came to find out that the answer to these questions is yes.

He shared that when the heart is broken, many times our spirit, will and confidence are also broken. This state of brokenness in essence, strips you of who you were. On the other hand, when one gets re-acquainted with love, the spirit re-emerges with renewed healing, one slowly regains the drive and the will to rise, our confidence soars and we rediscover ourselves, we re-discover that there is still something within us worth sharing.

CHAPTER 4
A NOTE ON TEMPTATION

As my personal search continued, there were quite a few thoughts that lingered in my mind, especially in the quiet moments. In the ensuing chapters, you will find my perspectives on relationships and how my growth transformed my thinking regarding things that I had learned in the past. Allow it to bring about growth in your thinking also. In the process, you may quite possibly gain deeper insights than I have.

I start off with Temptation. I have realized that it strikes mostly at the time of our hunger. I have had firsthand knowledge of this truth. I had to ask myself these questions, "What is it inside of me that longs to be filled? Is it affection? Attention? Do I desire a sense of belonging? Do I crave love? I had to be true to myself and admit that when my desires went unmet, I got vulnerable and found that that was the time that I was weak.

I learnt a couple of helpful strategies during the process and decided to share some tips that I believe can help:
1) Get closer to wholesome activities. Doing personal devotions is good but I believe that human interaction is crucial. Getting involved in a ministry or a voluntary organization helps to keep your mind more engaged and it also lifts your spirit just by being around others. You will become strengthened through fellowship and receive encouragement. Additionally you will meet new people which will do you a world of good socially.
2) Get active. Whether it is at work, going out, having hobbies or hanging with friends. You know what they say about the devil and idle hands. Get up and do

something!

3) Go to sleep early. This may sound like a joke but it works. It helps in the 9:00p.m. to 12:00a.m. hours when one can be distracted by the computer or telephone. Setting an early bed-time creates a regimen that soon your friends will come to respect. Most importantly, it lessens the chance for you doing or saying things you may regret later, in addition, you get restful sleep which will help make you feel refreshed in the morning.

4) Redeem the time. When you eventually meet someone you like, have an open discussion about your desires. Intentionally plan activities so that you won't just sit around each other's houses. Whether it's your first time or not, deliberately focus your time on building the friendship first. Now in this day and age I know that's tricky. Some of your male friends may say to you "You have one life to live, live it", and, yes, even while reading this you may be saying "Really now, she has got to be joking, that's going to take a long time and my clock is ticking!" Trust me, spending the time to build a strong foundation is worth it.

Ask yourself what is most important to you. If it is to experience a fulfilling solid relationship, then frivolous flings won't yank your chain. You will find these kinds of relationships as shallow and fleeting and frankly, a complete waste of time. The fact is, these kinds of relationships can be exciting for the moment, but they are very much in contrast to the pleasures of emotional ecstasy found in a more deep rooted commitment. This kind of relationship delivers far more substance and a whole lot more satisfaction.

CHAPTER 5
READY FOR LOVE OR READY TO LOVE

I am ready for love. Many persons have said this statement at some point in their lives, usually after a period of growing up, of loneliness or after the passing of yet another birthday and thinking that the biological clock is about to stop ticking and "I still don't gat a man!"

What does "I am ready for love" really mean though? I have found that in many cases, individuals who repeat this phrase are really saying that they feel ready for married life because they are either in good financial or educational standing, they have "come of age" or in some cases, it's because they believe their age is "almost off the calendar"- meaning, too old to mention! In retrospect, I have realized that many of them really meant that they were ready to receive love, not realizing that it also meant a lot of giving also.

Usually my girlfriends really meant that they thought was high time for them to get married, hardly stopping to ask themselves if they were ready to be a wife. I have found that there is a distinct difference. Being married is a status but choosing to be a wife or a husband is a state of mind. The real question that one should ask oneself is "Am I the marrying kind?" Let's face it, some of us aren't. The propelling force that gets you to that state of mind is love. Not the frivolous kind of love but the Corinthians kind. If you listen to the popular song by India Arie, bearing a similar title as this chapter, you will see that she touches on the other aspects of love that too many of us ignore. It speaks of the realities of the joys and pains of love and the need for an individual to be willing to learn and grow in the experience. The unfortunate truth is that some of us are not willing to go through that.

1 Corinthians 13:4-8 outlines clearly the attributes of love and with it implies that a committed heart and mind is needed to achieve this. This commitment comes with the possibilities of being hurt because, I re-iterate, we are in relationships with human beings who are prone to disappoint. Yet in the midst of disappointment, this commitment can also unearth the possibilities of joyous moments. Therein lies true love; the ability to remain committed regardless.

You may be thinking "Okay so this is where Superman and Wonder-Woman step in, for only super heroes or super humans can achieve this feat!" I submit to you that it only takes two committed hearts to make it work and two minds resolving to be in tune with each other and God.

According to Erich Fromm (1956), in his classic book, The Art of Loving, he declares that "To love somebody is not just a strong feeling, it is a decision, it is a judgment, it is a promise. If love were just a feeling, there would be no basis for the promise to love each other forever."

Dr. James Dobson (2004) conveys a similar message in his book Romantic Love: ".... a couple's love is not defined by the highs and lows, but is dependent on a commitment of their will. Stability comes from this irrepressible determination to make a success of marriage and to keep the flame aglow regardless of the circumstances."

I've always heard it said that love is a verb. It requires willful action on the part of individuals in order for it to be realized. It also encompasses the act of giving and receiving between persons. Where some of us go wrong is entering into marriage not realizing the amount of giving that will be required. Instead we look at what we will get out of it. It really is all about the giving of oneself into the life of another with the aim of helping to make that individual better, thus strengthening the bond between both. Understanding that it is dangerous to base a relationship on emotional highs or sexual euphoria is one of the first things a couple should grasp. If ignored, the couple will quickly discover that success in their relationship will be a fleeting dream and disillusionment will eventually emerge. Now I know that many of you have heard this before. Knowing is one thing. It's the doing that creates a challenge for many.

I've asked a few friends and acquaintances about their opinions on whether they believed that people were still open to the idea of doing what was necessary to build a successful marriage. I even took it a step further to ask whether they thought that the whole marriage concept was still seen as desirable in today's world. My questions stemmed from the fact that I had seen growing level of nonchalance from individuals, especially men, who had grown quite comfortable with having flings or had no desire for marriage at all. For many of them, jobs and extra-curricular activities took the place of building a deep relationship with someone because many of them thought that it took too much time and energy. Some had also been hurt and had no desire to risk being hurt again.

In other instances, many were already married but have

developed a sense of lethargy and, as such, their marriages just dragged along. My take is, neither situation is ideal. Making the effort to build a life with someone successfully is far more fulfilling than living alone and satisfying one's selfish sexual desires now and then. A healthy relationship where both understand how to truly love is beneficial to not only the union but to the individual also as the act of living unselfishly strengthens character.

There was a general consensus among my conversational partners though, that there is still hope and there are persons who still hold to the idea of experiencing the pleasures of a deep committed relationship. The challenge is to find them.

CHAPTER 6
THOUGHTS ON SUBMISSION

Submission of a woman to her husband has nothing to do with her being his doormat but more to her understanding of a biblical truth to a happy marriage. Statistics report that women have out-achieved men in terms of academics in recent years and have increased their earning capacity to be almost on par with men in the last 10 to 15 years, Forbes Magazine 2013. As a result, women have gained experience and knowledge that has made them more career-oriented and less domestic-minded. Given this information you may ask, how does a woman like that submit to a man who, in her mind, knows less than she does? How can she respect such a man and the decisions he makes, especially when she has been "Miss Independent" and used to making her own decisions ever since she became of age?

I've come to understand that the term submission does not mean that your voice is silenced in your relationship, but rather it means understanding how to respectfully give your opinion and leaving it alone thereafter. Practicing this brings a greater chance for mutual understanding in the relationship. If you're involved with a man who thinks his opinion is always the right one, understanding this point is even more important. The thing is, a man needs to feel that he is the problem solver and that he knows what's best for himself, you, the children, the dog, the cat and just about everything else (okay so I may be stretching it a bit). Always make sure though that your voice is heard and your ideas and suggestions are noted. Do this in a non-threatening manner and never with an attitude. If you don't take note of your tone, your man will feel threatened and eventually shut you out. Just state your thoughts and then leave it alone.

Even when you feel deep down that he is making the wrong decision or you feel that his stance is flawed, silence is required at this point. "Wha Wha Whaaaat? Did she just say that?" Let's think about it. The more you push your point, the greater the chance for an argument and for the chance of him never wanting to hear your suggestions or viewpoint again.

Leaving it alone is part of the submission process. If it means, biting your tongue, removing yourself physically or mentally from the situation or becoming engaged in another activity, then do it, but only after your voice is heard. Once he makes the decision or insists on maintaining his opinion, you have to resolve within yourself not to make a comment. I know it's hard especially when he decides to follow his own leading, but this is the time when you have to try to resist feeling resentful. Your silence is golden. Believe me! After a couple times of dealing with matters like this, the chances are great that he may change the way he thinks. He, in his own time, may realize that many times you were right, and that even after his decisions blew up in his face, you didn't rub it in, and, during the process, you were silent.

Your silence gave him respect and he will love you for that. Even with his ill-advised decisions or myopic opinions, you allowed him to see the error of his ways by himself and you were kind about it. That's deep!

After a while, he will accept your ideas and suggestions more easily and not feel threatened. He may even admit that you're better at some things and both of you agreeing that you are placed in charge of a specific decision-making process. Ladies, even when you have achieved this victory, it still requires you to respect him and not gloat about how much better you are at doing certain things. That would be most unwise.

In the name of achieving peace, women are constantly reminded of the submissive role they should take. As ladies, we often-times are asked to relinquish our right just to end an argument. "Give up your right for peace sake", I often heard my Mom say. As a child though, I had a warm time trying to figure out who the heck was "Pete?" but seriously though, if I were given a hundred dollars the many times I did that, I would be a very rich woman. I've recognized that when an argument brews, it is the woman who is usually expected to give in first. Now you may ask "Why is that?" "Surely there must be cases where he must give in too". Well after years of struggling and totally resenting the feeling that my voice was the one that was mostly silenced, I realized that I wasn't the only woman who felt this way. I noticed that because women felt this way, we ended up carrying feelings of anger in our hearts because we thought that our say was disregarded or ignored in our relationships. This resentment has to be dealt with and should never be ignored. Otherwise, it will only lead to increased tension in the relationship. Communication at this point is key. Both should be allowed to express their opinion with each respecting the other's thoughts sincerely.

It is true that there are men who, no matter how many times their single-handed decisions and deep-set views have been proven wrong, hardly admit their error. With arrogance as a flaw, they may not entertain open communication. Submission to a man like this will no doubt be difficult. The thing is, you really should have known the man to whom you were committing before doing so. No-one wants to be treated like as a doormat, so doing the necessary preparation before making a long-term commitment is advisable. Take time to observe him in various situations, note the way he responds to things. You will most likely find his true character emerging naturally even though he may try to suppress it in a bid to impress you. One more thing, when his inner self is revealed, be honest with yourself. Don't ignore the red flags. If you find that you cannot handle some of the character traits that are revealed, walk away. Remember, I am talking about the deal breakers not simple traits that can be ignored. These are character tendencies that negatively affect your concept of self, your self-esteem and self- worth.

Here's a tip, discuss this issue before committing to each other. Note his stance as it relates to his authority, wifely submission, decision-making roles within the family, the valuing of each other's opinions, his opinion on a woman who has achieved more in life than her mate and his overall respect of women. Another tip, watch how he treats the women in his life; his mother, sisters and aunts. That will give you good indicators as to how he will treat you. The answers to these will definitely give you an idea of who he is.

Submission shouldn't be regarded as a duty but rather something done by a woman because she trusts her man to not abuse her position of vulnerability. If he loves you, he will never take advantage of your willingness to submit. It is easier to give up your right to a man who respects and loves you than to one who doesn't.

But wait, there is another side; the bible also speaks about submitting to each other.

Ephesians 5:21
"Submit to one another out of reverence to Christ"
New International Version (NIV)

This scripture reminds us that submission is required by all out of reverence to God. Submission is therefore a two-way street where the wife understands her role in submission and the husband understands his as well. When both individuals understand that submission is not done to put ourselves down but rather to build up the one to whom the act of submission is rendered, the union is then strengthened. In so doing, the relationship, on the whole is therefore strengthened, since no one seeks self-glory but rather takes the interest of others into consideration. Submission should therefore not be considered as a bad word but rather a position of empowerment that facilitates the strengthening of a commitment between persons, providing that each embraces the concept and willingly participate in the process.

CHAPTER 7
PART I
ONE MAN FOR ONE WOMAN?... HMMM

So here's my theory; I believe that God has created someone that best fits you as a mate. Note that I didn't say that He has created a perfect mate for you and neither did I say that there is only one person for you. These ideas are not only absurd but laughable in my opinion. What I mean is that I believe that He knows the person who will fit in with your idiosyncrasies and character traits and who will be (okay if I really have to use the word) perfect for you. Nowhere in this sentence am I saying that the person will be perfect, as in, having no faults or flaws, because no human is without flaws. Rather, I am saying that I hold the belief that there is someone who will find it easiest to deal with and love you, just the way you are.

Further to this belief is my opinion that God also knows that there will be others with whom you will be able to connect and that they too can be a good fit for you with a little more effort. God has given us the freedom of choice and guidance in His word. When you choose your lifelong mate, regardless of whether he is the best fit for you in God's eyes, God expects you to keep your commitment. He is very much aware that in your lifetime you may quite likely meet others that you will also have a connection with, but He watches to see what you will do when you meet them. The point is, it is a fact that you will be attracted to more than one person in life, but I believe there is only one person that is the best fit for you, even though others may come close.

There are those who are blessed to have found their best fit, their best friends, and made them their spouse. They have experienced love at its best, even with the ups and downs. Others have made spouses of the ones with whom they only connected with on certain levels. God's requirement for us is to make both types of relationships work, and they can! Admittedly, the effort would be easier with the one who fits you best, who is most compatible with you, who shares similar goals, aspirations and viewpoints on spirituality and life itself.

Ideally, taking the time to find your best fit pays off. It makes the journey a whole lot easier. In that way, when you have found your best fit and then meet others you're attracted to, the challenge become easier to fight, because the connection between yourself and your mate is much stronger than the temptation. If, on the other hand, you marry someone with some of the qualities you are attracted to, and then meet someone else with whom you are more compatible, the challenge becomes greater, albeit not impossible.

Take the time to find your best fit and then make that person your best friend. Remember though, whomever you choose to marry, God still expects you to remain committed to your partner. However, marrying someone to whom you are best suited will ensure that you would have married the one with whom you are most compatible and to whom you are most attracted. Chances of success in this type of relationship will then be far greater than in others.

You may ask how one can determine if they have found

their best fit. I believe that life gives us warnings and red flags that are meant to alert us to possible areas of conflict and unease in our relationships. The less red flags and the comfort one experiences in a solid unrushed relationship, despite the emotional highs and lows, the greater the indication that you may have found your best fit. Take your time though and consider the possibility that he may not be the first man that tickles your fancy. Go out, meet as many persons as possible and be open to widening your horizons and chances of finding your best.

CHAPTER 7
Part II
A THOUGHT ON MONOGAMY

I suggested to a friend of mine the following opinion: A good man is one who tries to understand and care for his woman, whose main desire is to love God, and be faithful to his wife and family. I also suggested that a woman is blessed if she found a man like that. My friend's funny response was "Is there such a man still living?" Without missing a beat I said "Of course!" Now I wasn't quite sure if he was hoping the conversation would continue so as to provide him with the opportunity to show himself as such an example, but my mind took a turn towards a deeper contemplation on the topic.

I had realized then and even now that I seem to have fallen in the minority who believe that relationships should be monogamous. In fact, I read quite recently a writer's blog who shared the view that marriage and monogamy is a farce. The author based his argument on the intrinsic insatiable sexual nature of men that makes it almost impossible for him to be satisfied by one woman. He made references to significant leaders in the bible and in history who had many wives.

While all of this may be true, I still believe that it is possible and that God equipped us to achieve it. If it were impossible for us to succeed at it, then why would His Word support marriage or the union of a man and a woman as ideal? A mistake? I don't think so.

While I spoke with my friend, I found it quite funny that I probably came across as extremely naïve to be expecting that there still exists a man who desired to settle down with one woman. We've heard the clichés; "nowadays men can't be faithful, every man has to have a girl on the side, women now have to settle with sharing their men". While I know the possibilities of a successful relationship in today's world may seem grim, I still believe that an individual can find a partner with whom compatibility exists and a contented life can be their reality.

A very important point must be made here. I am not proposing or promising that he/she will never cheat, disappoint or hurt you and I am not saying that one person can fulfill all your needs. I am rather saying that I believe that there are individuals who still have the desire to have solid and beautiful relationships with one partner. Finding that person is a blessing and not an impossibility.

CHAPTER 8
MAKE HIM FEEL LIKE A KING

I remember distinctly being in church one Sunday listening to an interesting presentation by the guest speaker on a Ladies' Sunday gathering. Now this speaker would not have been considered a great orator, because she was not blessed with eloquence and sensational words, but rather she was a humble woman with a soft voice, but even through her simplicity, had the congregants hanging on to her every word. I'm now forgetting the actual topic, but I remember though that it was surrounding the theme, Becoming a Good Wife. Her approach was from a personal perspective where she shared how God had spoken to her years before to change the way she treated and responded to her husband.

She shared how she learned to greet him at the door with a kiss (she was a house-wife), to take his shoes off as he sat in his chair, ensure that dinner was ready, that she was freshly showered and smelling good, that she sat by him and asked him about his day before sharing her day and that she was never out of his presence for too long unless mutually agreed. "Say whaaaattt?" Indeed, many of us younger girls back then found her words to be a big joke. I can also imagine some of you reading this saying "She must be kidding, things and times have changed. Which woman has time to wait on her man hand and foot!"

Now years have passed and I have found that many of the points that the speaker had shared can be seen as practical and sensible advice. Okay, so nowadays, both women and men go out to work so the chances of a woman reaching home before her man, long enough for her to shower, cook and then meet him at the door with a kiss are pretty slim. What jumped out at me though, was the importance of paying attention to him.

From talking to friends and other married persons, I have learnt that for a relationship to survive and thrive, training yourself to focus on your partner is crucial. Notice I said train, because even though it is such a small word, it takes great effort with all of life's distractions bombarding us daily, to consciously ensure that your mate is given priority.

So how exactly do we do this? Making him feel like a king covers a wide range of issues. Issues of sex, doing things you don't want to, respecting him when sometimes it's hard to, are just some examples. Speaking of sex ladies, I'm not just talking about the act. Men need a little more than just your presence. He wants to feel that you are completely involved in the process and that you desire him. This is especially true when you feel tired and your first instinct is to say "Not tonight!" Sometimes you have to pick up on his signals during the evening and then try to find time to freshen up, drink some coffee, tea, or whatever else works for you in order to perk yourself up, especially when you have said "not tonight" for the past few nights. Also remember that your initiation is very necessary in showing him that you are very much interested and connected to him physically. Your efforts would be treasured as you make him feel loved. Of course all in good reason, as your mate ought to be considerate in understanding that rest is important.

Other concerns include doing things you don't want to do but doing them anyway but it makes him happy. Oh boy now that's a challenge! Imagine you are on your way home and you both get into an argument. The way you are angry you probably would curdle the food if you attempt to cook dinner. So your first thought is "mek him guh nyam bulla and cheese ya man!" (let him eat bun and cheese). Now with a re-conditioning of your mind over time, your second thought would be "let me cool off a bit and still fix dinner the way he likes it". Doing this may require a great amount of will power. Not only may it require you to shower about two more times before you really cool down but it may also cause you to ask yourself "Is all this worth it though? Does going through all this to make him feel like a king ensure that he will treat me like his queen and that he won't be unfaithful?

Ensure? Now that's a strong word. You cannot ensure anything in life and you certainly can't ensure that your actions will make him your perfect husband. What your actions will do however, is re-affirm your love for your mate. It also shows your willingness to do what must be done to keep the fire going in your relationship. It is these selfless acts of love that he will remember when that pretty young thing at work tries to seduce him. If the man really loves you deeply, it will move him to refuse the propositions that he receives from other women and reciprocate acts of love towards you. Unless he is made of steel having no feelings, selfish or have no regard for the relationship, then he will make the effort to show you his appreciation, admiration and love.

I recently heard on a local radio programme, a speaker who shared how she learnt from her 5-year old daughter how to truly adore her husband, and how eventually it was reciprocated. She learned from her daughter how to give him sincere compliments, how to focus on his positives rather than negatives, how to be around him and how to give him physical affection. She admitted that she had to focus on doing this because she wanted to, and not because she was waiting for it to be given back, because waiting for reciprocation may bring frustration. I have found that if something is done with the intention of receiving, the individual may become disappointed because the expected returns may not materialize and resentment and anger then sets in.

I had realized a truth some time ago and the word of God confirmed it many times over.

Psalm 118:8
"It is better to trust in the LORD than to put confidence in man"

King James Version (KJV)

Now I had heard this scripture repeated many times but I received a greater illumination of the phrase about ten years ago. Simply put, we are commanded to love and submit to our mates but trust God. This is because, as humans, you and your mate have flaws, faults, idiosyncrasies and vices. Therefore placing trust in a human being is laced with the possibility of disappointment. Let me state clearly that trust is important in relationships. It creates stability and an atmosphere of openness. However, placing ultimate trust in a spouse and oneself for the success of a marriage is unwise. That level of trust should be directed to God as He is the one who will help each partner to be the best partner possible.

I have learnt that we have to trust God to help our mates be good partners. Trust God to help your partner be a good lover, support, spiritual encourager and friend for life. Now, as I indicated before, God's ability to keep your relationship is irrefutable whether it lasts or not. However, a man's choice is always based on his free will. So if your mate makes negative choices, you cannot help that. Therefore, in learning how to adore your mate, you have to genuinely do it, trusting that she, by the help of God, will truly reciprocate this love and affection. One thing is clear in this revelation, and this is that your mate, in order to be the partner they ought to be, needs to be at the place where she is hearing from God. I have realized that you must be connected to your partner on a spiritual, emotional and physical level, in that order. Now, I respect all marriages, whether they are built on spiritual grounds or not, but I am convinced though that it is a bit harder to keep it lasting if both partners are not spiritually connected to each other and to God.

A recent US study indicated that the strongest marriages, do not involve two persons who look to each other for happiness. Instead, the research revealed that those who said they put God at the center of their marriage were far more likely to be at the highest level of happiness. They weren't looking to a spouse (or to marriage) for something that only God can deliver. Look to Him for fulfillment, first. Matthew 6:31-33 reminds us that God knows our needs whether they are physical, emotional or spiritual, and that if we seek Him first, He will supply all our needs. Removing that pressure from your spouse may be just what your relationship needs to thrive.

CHAPTER 9
MY THOUGHTS ON MEN

These are my opinions and not gospel. As you read, maybe you will see similarities in the way you see men.

- Men most times express their feelings through the things they value. If he shares with you what he values, value it too because it means that he regards you highly or loves you.

- Men usually live out male stereotypes but really are as vulnerable as you are and also need emotional support.

- Men need to feel that they are always in control, the problem-solver, the one who comes up with the best decisions. Offer your opinions but show him your respect also.

- Men are fearful of being seen as inferior, inadequate or undesirable. You need to ensure that he knows that you find him desirable and that you are proud of him and his efforts.

- If physical encounters are limited, a simple hug could spell SEX to him. That's just the way he is wired. Plus they are visual beings, so a sexually starved man enticed by a visual image, will more than likely lead to misguided actions on his part. The matter of fidelity and what it means to both of you will therefore have to be discussed. In this way, both of you will know what each other can do to prevent infidelity.

- They say men are from Mars and women are from Venus. However, no matter how different we are, I believe that once there is compatibility between each other, a mutual commitment to stay together and a mutual understanding that God must be at the centre, then success is possible.

CHAPTER 10
WHAT TYPE IS HE?

While I do understand that no individual will perfectly fall into a specific mold or "type" classification, I was once inspired by a presentation I had attended some years ago which dealt with understanding the type of man you are attracted to.

In seeking the partner that best fits you, here are my notes that may help you in your quest:

1. The Unmarried/Happily Single - he is devoted to his job, his friends or church. It would take someone special to catch his attention. Someone with much more than just a pretty face and a fantastic shape would be needed for this contented single man to turn his head in your direction.

2. The Kingdom Seeker- he is the one who (whether he is a Christian or not) desires to seek God's will for his life. He believes in marriage and putting God first especially in the pursuit of his life partner.

3. The Realist- He recognizes the worth of a woman in his life and does not take advantage of her. He desires to please her and he shows his regard and respect for her long before the dating stage.

4. The Learner- He is constantly in pursuit of knowledge not just academically but is also open to gain knowledge about love and how to have a successful relationship.

5. The Multiplier- He constantly adds to you and his presence multiplies your potential. He complements your life through his values, his encouragement and his constant support.

6. The Servant- He has a pattern of submitting to authority. Don't get me wrong, he is not a "softie" or a "wimp" but rather he has the wisdom to know when to be silent and learn. This trait will help him understand how to submit to God as the sustainer and head of his life and subsequently, he will learn how to commit and remain committed to his mate.

7. The Consistent Man- He is in no rush because he does not have poor intentions toward his woman. He is not interested in manipulating her and then leaving. He is in it for the long haul. A woman may regard this man as "slow", especially when she believes that her "age papers" are lost or are almost totally destroyed in the flames of time. To many women, this man seems not to understand their plight, and most times, is regarded as the man to avoid. This may be a mistake though as he may very well be the diamond in the rough.

Which type are you attracted to? A better question is who is your best fit? Remember these are not molds to fit your partner into, but rather a guide to help you understand the type of person he is. Also, there are other trait-types I am sure others can come up with, so this list is by no means exhaustive. He, more than likely, will exhibit more than one of these traits. The aim is to understand him and determine how he complements you.

CHAPTER 11
HELPFUL TIPS, WRITE THEM DOWN

Over the years I have subscribed to awesome inspirational sites and read and benefited from several books and articles written by well -known authors. It is my hope that you too will be changed for the better as I share my notes on insights that I have gained.

COMMUNICATION

Achieving good communication is crucial in any relationship. Take note of these the next time you speak to your mate:

1) Make sure your body language, facial expressions and vocal tone are in line with your message.
2) Be honest, direct and focus on the real issue. If you can't come up with a definitive solution, at least try to end the conversation on a positive note like "I'm glad we talked. Let's continue to talk about it tomorrow and try to come up with a better solution."
3) Don't ever be rude or talk down to your mate/spouse. Don't dismiss an idea or thought as absurd, but instead listen to their point and then react with the reasons you disagree in a respectful manner.
4) Stay on track. If you sit down to talk about a financial problem and suddenly other emotional issues are coming up, realize that you may need to focus on one area at a time in order to create solutions instead of mere bickering.

5) Recognize when you may need outside help to communicate effectively. A counselor or marriage retreat may help solve what seems to be an impossible communication problem.

MOVING TOWARDS A BETTER RELATIONSHIP

1) When your partner comes into the room, try putting down whatever you're doing and verbally express your delight at seeing them. This simple gesture can mean so much to both of you.

2) Observe the red flags in your relationship and be honest about what you can deal with. It's almost pointless to question how your spouse processes things, or why he does what he does or acts the way he does. First, asking questions of this nature is redundant since he is the way he is. The point is, it is up to YOU to decide whether you can live with it. Preferably, you should have decided this before committing. Secondly, trying to change your mate is absurd and almost impossible, so "Forget about it". A friend once said to me "You cannot alter a man at the altar". That saying hit the nail on the head as I realized that it really is up to an individual to decide whether she can or cannot deal with a certain trait or habit of their partner.

3) Again, try to know your mate well before marriage and remember, be honest. If you don't think you can deal with certain idiosyncrasies he may have, it's better not to enter into lifelong commitment. Men, the same applies to you. Let me add an important point. Helping your mate get over self-destructive habits or negative traits is a positive reinforcement of your love for your partner. What I am referring to

specifically under this topic, are traits that are simple enough to ignore and habits that can be dealt with. For some, they can succeed at overlooking these drawbacks in their mate, for others, it's an uphill task. The point is, be true to your feelings about what it is you can deal with and make that decision before making a commitment.

4) Protect your own heart. Love yourself fully but there is a special place in your heart where no one must enter except for your partner. Keep that space always ready to receive and invite your mate in, and refuse to let anyone or anything else enter there.

5) Fall in love over and over again. You will constantly change. You're not the same persons you were when you first met, and in five years you will not be the same person you are today. Change will come, and in that you have to re-choose each other every day. The important point here is that it is a choice to love and to remain in love even in the midst of change. Each individual has to believe that their commitment will remain unchanged even though their individual lives have changed in some way or another. It's not your job to change or fix your partner. Your job is to love her as she is. If she changes, embrace the evolution of your mate, grow alongside her because you don't want her to outgrow you.

6) Never stop growing together. The stagnant pond breeds malaria but a flowing stream is always fresh and cool. Atrophy is the natural process when you stop working a muscle, just as it is if you stop working on your relationship. Find common goals, dreams and visions to work towards.

7) Always see the best in each other. Focus only on what you love in your partner. If you focus on what annoys you, you will always see the negative. If you focus on what you love, you will find it easier to continue loving your partner. You will also reduce the possibility of the temptation of comparing your mate with someone else.

8) Take full accountability for your own emotions. It's not your mate's job to make you happy, and your sadness is up to you. You are responsible for finding your own happiness, and through that your joy will spill over into your relationship.

9) Allow your mate to just be. Men, when your woman is sad or upset, it's really not your job to fix it, it's your job to hold her and let her know you're there and that it's okay. It's a nice gesture to try and help but most times, she just wants you to let her know that you hear her, and that she's important and that she can always lean on you. As you remain strong and un-judging she will trust you and open her soul to you. Be present and strong and let her know you aren't going anywhere. Listen to what she is really saying behind the words and emotion. Be present. Give her not only your time, but your focus, your attention and your soul. Do whatever it takes to clear your head so that when you are with her you are fully with her. Treat her as you would your most valuable client. She is.

10) Give her space. Sometimes she will need to be reminded to take time to nurture herself. Tell her to take time for herself, especially after you have children. She needs that space to renew and get re-centered, and to find herself after she gets lost in serving you and the children. This 'me' time is

important to her because this is also the time that she focuses not just on her emotional needs but on her physical needs as well. In so doing, you will benefit as you will have a woman who is happy, healthy, in shape and ready to be the woman that you need her to be.

11) Learn to be silly. Do not take yourself and life so seriously. Laugh. Laughter makes dealing with everything else (which includes the rough times) easier.

12) Be fully transparent. If you want to have trust you must be willing to share everything, especially those things you don't want to share. It takes courage to fully love, to fully open your heart and let someone in when you don't know whether they will like what they will find. Part of that courage is allowing that person to love you completely, your darkness as well as your light. Drop the mask. If you feel like you need to wear a mask, you will never experience the full dimension of what love can be.

13) Be vulnerable. You don't have to have it all together. Be willing to share your fears and feelings, and quick to acknowledge your mistakes. On a quick note, sharing your past with your partner is your choice. My opinion is that this should be carefully contemplated before action is taken since you cannot predict how well your partner will handle it. Be wise. The past should remain in the past especially if it is no longer pertinent to your present. If it is, then it is up to you.

14) Forgive immediately and focus on the future rather than carrying weight from the past. Don't let your history hold you hostage. Holding onto past mistakes that either you or she makes, is like a heavy anchor to your marriage and will hold you back. Forgiveness is freedom. Remember we all did things we may not have been proud of in the past so don't judge. Focus on moving forward instead.

15) Always choose love. If this is the guiding principle through which all your choices are made, there is nothing that will threaten the happiness of your marriage. Love will always endure.

16) Remember in the end, marriage isn't about happily ever after. It's about effort and a commitment to grow together and a willingness to continually invest in creating something that can last. Through that work, the happiness will come. Learning to learn from and love each experience, will bring a deeper understanding of your relationship, thereby strengthening and continually affirming your bond with each other.

HAVING AFFAIRS

Some people have affairs because they tell themselves that they deserve more attention than they get at home. Or maybe they get annoyed because they feel that all of their needs aren't getting met by their partner. Hmmm, where did we get the idea that one person could meet our every need? I believe that it is actually quite possible for two individuals to live comfortably without having all of their needs met. If you think about it this way you might be surprised how liberating it is. You are not perfect, and neither is your partner, but you can make a very happy life together if you are both serious about providing the love and support that go along with a good union.

Maybe you want your spouse to be like you. The truth is, many factors account for the differences between both of you; family background, cultural variations, temperament. God could have created clones if He wanted spouses to be carbon copies of each other. Instead He wants you both to appreciate each other's unique qualities and create an atmosphere of blended unity.

Instead of trying to make your mate "see things your way," you can benefit from having different perspectives. Blend your views to see things more accurately than either of you could individually. It's not unreasonable to want your needs met. But it is unreasonable to see your spouse as your private genie.

MAKING TIME TO MAKE LOVE
Many girlfriends can agree when I say that we use the excuse of being too busy or too tired to be romantic. I have spoken to many men on this topic and it all boils down to this: men crave sexual attention. Sex is very important to them, and we are not talking about just sex, we are talking about sex with a little spice. Ladies, you know what I mean. Now, I am not proposing that women become expert contortionists or sex machines, but rather learn techniques that can pleasantly surprise their mates.

Therefore ladies, unless you work on a construction site, run a multi-national corporation or are engaged in excessive manual labour making you completely worn out at the end of the day, your excuses to connect intimately with your partner may mean that you have just lost sight of your priorities. I have discovered that if you wish to stay connected and happy in your marriage, never be too tired or too busy to feel love for your partner. When your life is nearly over, you will regret it if you look back and recall the many nights when you made excuses instead of making love.

FROM LOVERS TO PARENTS

It's true that when your babies are small, there isn't much time left over for romantic gestures. But the wonderful thing about romance is that it is the quality, never the quantity that matters. So when the baby is napping, be creative and rekindle that amorous feeling for your mate. Write love notes to each other and slip them in places that are unexpected. Be innovative, and if you want your love to flourish, it certainly will.

ADJUSTING DURING MONEY PROBLEMS

The most important ingredient for getting through tough economic times is the truth. The other ingredient is maturity. This is not the time to sulk about a lowered standard of living or choosing to ignore the real situation and live at the same standard that you are used to. An extended period of income loss sometimes calls for sacrifice. It may mean taking the children out of preparatory schools and placing them instead a public primary school for some time. If you are renting, it may mean finding a cheaper alternative. How an individual reacts to the loss of a job depends a lot on their upbringing and level of maturity. It is always wise to discuss these matters before marriage because it has been known that financial hardship in a relationship sometimes is a major factor in its demise. While going through it, however, be honest with your partner and together make a plan for dealing with your debts and your spending.

TUNING IN TO YOUR PARTNER

Life is complicated and can be exhausting, so there is always a temptation when you get home to tune out, because for many, home is place where you should feel safe enough to let your guard down. I have come to understand though that there is a difference between relaxing and disengaging, and, while relaxing is a healthy way to recharge your mental and spiritual batteries, disengaging puts a drain on you and your relationship. It is extremely important to recognize the difference and stay present for all the people you love. For example, you want to watch TV, watch TV together hugging, cuddling, even if it is in silence. The effect of your physical presence is far reaching as it engenders closeness and intimacy.

BRINGING UP THE PAST

Do not rehash the past. Once a problem is solved, that's it. This is a very liberating feeling as it gives you a sense of progress in your relationship and shows that you are beginning to understand each other in a more meaningful way.

CONTROLLING YOUR ANGER

When you're ready to blow, you might say anything, hurtful things you would normally spare the person you love from hearing. Don't say something you'll regret forever. Don't give your partner an excuse to come back to you with his or her own resentments. Instead, find a way to get your anger under control. Do or say something silly or do whatever little trick that helps bring you outside of yourself long enough to regain control. Humour most times works like a charm. Be careful not to come across as making light of the situation because that may make matter worse. For some, walking away works best.

CHAPTER 12
MOM'S GONE

September 25, 2010. My mommy died today at 8:45p.m. I had prayed before "please God don't make her suffer". That was my secret prayer that I had shared with no-one. I am thankful that God answered my prayer. Even though I wanted her to remain with us much longer, I had decided within myself that if it meant her writhing in pain much longer, then I would ask God to grant her the shortest possible period of suffering. It was approximately five months between the initial diagnosis and her death. Pretty fast I would say, and although I am still amazed at the swift turn of events, I have accepted it.

Even now though, I am still a bit at a loss for words as to how fast it all went. I still remember the times I took her to the hospital, her look of hope and bravery. I remember being with her after the hospital visits and on weekends. Every visit was basically the same; making sure she was comfortable, she had food nearby, her Ensure was handy and most importantly, her bible and inspirational booklet was beside her. She never allowed us to be around her with a sad face, so I made every effort to remain cheerful. Someone was at home with her during the week, and on the times that we could not be there, we always checked in on her progress. Mom knew it was hard for us as caregivers. My sister and I were in demanding jobs, I was going through a divorce and there was hardly anyone there who could physically help. I still thank God though for the job I was in and for the understanding boss that I had at the time. Not every company would have allowed their employee to leave work for approximately 4 hours every other Tuesday to take their mother to the hospital for treatment.

I was there on the Saturday, earlier in the day. Dad was there but I got there about 10:00a.m., guilty that I could not have gotten there earlier to administer her early morning dose of pain relieving medication. I gave her the medication as soon as I came and put her in a colourful robe to refresh her. Every ten minutes Mom would groan and by then we all knew that that meant that she needed a shift in her position. I got a call from our Pastor requesting that he visit with her. Up until that time, Mom had made it quite clear that she had no desire to entertain visitors neither did she want her "story" to be told, so when our Pastor's request came, we had to make sure she was aware and was okay with it.

We had arranged for the nurse to be with her throughout that night and my sister was also to come for the evening shift on that day. Our Pastor came in the early evening and spoke to Dad for a while. By the time he was leaving, my sister, my nephew and a close member of the family had also come. We held hands around her bed and our Pastor prayed. I still remember my Mom looking around at all of us, now unable to speak and eyes glazed, but I believe she was quite aware of who was in the room and what we were doing. I thought at that time, Mom was ready.

The nurse came shortly after. Before I left, I kissed her and said "Love you Mom". My nephew and I left. I stopped at the supermarket, dropped him home, reached home and then got the call. My sister in tears, couldn't get the words out. I kept asking her to tell me, while she cried uncontrollably. I knew what she was about to say but needed to hear it said. "Mommy's gone". I screamed "Oh Goddd" After crying together on the phone for a while, I started to say " Thank you Jesus, no more pain, no more pain, she's in no more pain, thank you!" It was then that I shared with my sister, my secret prayer of a short period of suffering for Mom.

I hung up the phone, turned right around and went through the door. I then picked up my nephew and we went back to the family home. We drove in silence. I got to the home and met my sister at the door. By that time some close church friends had come. I quietly walked to the room that I was in just earlier that day, and observed my Mom in the colourful robe that I had put on her. She was still of course, and I asked the nurse if she was sure that she was gone. She kept saying yes but I insisted that I saw signs of life "Didn't you see that a while ago? She just breathed, didn't you see it? ". She looked at me with sympathetic eyes and shook her head. It was then I just stopped and stared. I walked over and touched her. She was gone.

God has proven himself to be a healer many times in the past. People's testimonies speak of it over and over again. However, I had to re-affirm that if He had chosen not to heal my mother, he was still, irrefutably, a healer. I believe Mom knew everyone who came to help, who meant well, even though we may have let her down in meeting all her needs during her ordeal. I believe though that she knew that it was also hard on us to see her suffering.

Mom was brave. I believe that even though she held on for a healing miracle, she was not angry that it didn't happen, because at some point, she accepted that maybe, possibly, this could have been her time to go. Some may say we did not have enough faith, others may say it was just her time. While I still ponder on this, I reflect on her life. In life she put my efforts to shame. She was such an example of a faithful servant in life and in death. I have to try a little harder, do a little better. To this day, I still thank God for granting Mom a peaceful transition.

Fear of death

I do get a little freaked out at the thought of death sometimes, but in retrospect, I realize that it is more the pain that comes with it that I loathe. Don't we all?

While my Mom groaned, I used to ask myself "Why does pain have to come along with death? "Of course I know that there are instances of death where seemingly there is little or no pain and I could have thought of many examples, but at that time, I was only focusing on Mom's anguish.

I have come to understand that death is transitory, a path that must be trodden in order to prepare us for our judgment. The greater focus then becomes "Am I ready?" "Have I done my best?" "Have I fulfilled my purpose?" Since we can't do anything about it, it makes no sense thinking about it. The greater focus should be on preparing ourselves on what happens after and ensuring that we are ready.

Our times together

Oh boy did we have our disagreements! I found out the reason for this a long time ago though. You see, even though I exhibited traits of my father, and some would say, I looked like him, truth is, I was very much like Mom. Many persons saw it; the tenacity, the charm, the wit, the humour, the fighting spirit, perseverance, inner strength and also opinionated. The thing is, we disagreed many times but I did listen to her advice and followed them, even though she thought I didn't. Sometimes it proved easier to agree to disagree.

In retrospect, I am mostly who I am today, because of my mother's example. I can finally stand on my own having gone through bad times with her there giving advice and offering tough love. I realized that it was also tough for my mother to see her daughters struggling and as a result, it propelled her many times to sacrifice and assist us in any way that she could. "Tough it up and stop feeling sorry for yourself" "It's not the end of the world, It's time to move on!" were some of the phrases I used to hear her say. She was the strongest woman I have ever known and I am grateful that she was my mother.

Lessons learnt:

1) Life is as grim or as grand as you make it, it's all up to your attitude. My mother taught me how to persevere through difficult times. She showed how one's mental perspective on situations can determine the outcome. I could have wallowed in self-pity many times, but Mom taught me how to smile at each storm and to keep moving on.

2) God expects us to remain faithful even to the end. Death is a hard pill to swallow usually, and is often followed by a lot of questions "Why Lord?" "Why her?" "Why now?" Many of us at times, curse God at the apparent injustice of an untimely death. This, I have found, is a test. For, who are we to determine when a death is untimely or not? Who are we to decide that it

was not the right time for death to come? We are asked to believe that God is in control and when death hovers, then we must believe that He knows what is best.

3) Death is really a transition. Everyone must die, we have to accept that. It is however, up to us, to determine what happens after.

CHAPTER 13
TRIBUTE TO MOM – ONE YEAR AFTER

A year ago and our world stood still, as we watched you bravely make your transition.
In disbelief, we cried ourselves to sleep at nights, remembering your voice of wisdom.

For it is appointed unto man once to die, we know the scripture well,
But when it swiftly came for you that night, the pain was too hard to tell.

We cherish the hope that we have not in vain, that we will see your face once again.
For you have left for us an example to follow, in your service to God and friends.

While the echo transcends the home that was yours and your family moves forward still,
We cry not for you, for your fate was fixed within the Master's will.

We cried…we mourned… life stood still it seemed, allowing us to grieve for a while.
Then we took our first steps without you, alone and somewhat afraid of what laid beyond the next mile.

We've gone a year without you, but life continues on. For God provides the comfort that continually makes us strong.
"Don't cry for me" you would say, "make sure you are there to stand…
With me when the Father says "Welcome home my child, come take my hand".

CHAPTER 14
IT'S MOVING TIME!

December 10, 2012. I moved into my new home today! God is indeed a gracious God, a provider and a way-maker. It was only two years ago that Mom had passed and I was now looking toward a new phase in my life, one that I had hoped I could have shared with her. I remember discussing with her and deciding what type of home I would have needed based on my stage of life and the situation that I was about to face. I knew that my life would require a home with little maintenance, offering the least amount of stress possible.

Managing a home that required gardening, excessive home and roof repairs, tree cutting during the hurricane season, flood and crime prevention mechanisms, or had too many entry and exit points, were too much for one woman to worry about. I actually requested from God the specific type of home I needed. An element of security also had to be present in my home community.

This "ideal home" at an affordable price looked more and more absurd as time passed, as I did my investigations as to what the going cost was for these types of homes. It was laughable actually, as the prices were far beyond my reach based on my earning power at the time. Sure there were neighbourhoods that I could have afforded at the time, but these communities were a bit "rough" to say the least.

The settlement to an ongoing matter had finally ended, and my final payout along with my contributions to the government's mortgage financier, left me looking for an average priced home. Looking at what was in my hand and the options that were out there, I knew I needed a miracle to find the home that I needed at an affordable price. I eventually saw a home in my neighbourhood that fit my needs but it was going for exactly $1M more than I could afford. I desperately tried to figure out how in the world I could afford this. Bottom line is that I couldn't, and eventually, someone else made an offer. Somehow though, I had the urge to drive to the community just to look. I drove in behind a car through the electronic gates and realized that this was exactly what I desired. I was pleasantly surprised that the community was nicely maintained and quiet.

The homes were small but perfect! What a pity the one that was available was already being sold. I soon saw a lady who was standing at her door and felt the urge to ask her if she knew of any units that were for sale. To my surprise she said "This one!" Not wanting to jump to conclusions, I wondered whether this was the same unit that I had seen online that was already in the process of sale. I then made an almost ridiculous request, "I know you don't know me but is it possible for me to have a look inside?" To my amazement she agreed.

Walking through the home I fell in love with it and knew that this was it. She had explained that she was taking care of the home for the owner but gave me the particulars to make contact. That very evening I called the owner in Bahamas, still wondering if this was the same house online. After a fairly short conversation, finally convinced that this was a different house, I asked for the selling price. I thought I had heard incorrectly and asked her to repeat when she quoted the exact amount of money I had as the selling price. Not fully accepting the miracle that was unfolding before my eyes, I asked whether she had already done a valuation. She confirmed and reiterated that the price was final. I hung up the phone amazed at how things had worked out.

At the end of this miraculous process, I got the mortgage for the remaining balance. Additionally, the closing costs inclusive of the other fees were all taken care of with my years of contributions to the government's mortgage financier. The resounding miracle is that I now own a home that requires little gardening, no excessive home and roof repairs, no need for tree cutting during the hurricane season, no need for flood or excessive crime prevention mechanisms, and not many entry and exit points. Further to that, I got this house with all that I had in my hand and nothing more.

Lesson learnt: Little is much when God is in it. He can work with all that you have to provide all that you need. Point to note, the valuation revealed that the home was valued for more than the selling price and the owner was aware. I bought it at the lowest value possible. In other words, I got the home that was perfect for my needs at the time, a home that I had specifically described to God; for all that I had in my hand and nothing more. Don't misread my words as boasting, just simple gratitude for His blessings.

CHAPTER 15
BE TRUE TO YOURSELF

"This above all, to thine own self be true"
William Shakespeare

I've realized a long time ago that I had lived most of my youth trying to please others. Up to age 25, I lived my life being concerned with people's opinions of me and my choices, and the thought of upsetting a norm caused by my confrontation or questions, brought me anxiety. I, as a result, stayed within the lines, avoided arguments and agreed with almost everything. Now, having an inquisitive mind from birth, willingly accepting other people's opinions was a little hard for me growing up. But guess what? I learnt to follow that advice and have admittedly benefitted from it in my relationships. Eventually though, what happened to me was that I ended up applying this approach to other aspects of my life and soon, I began quelling my individual thoughts, my query of other person's opinions, my inner desires and even my everyday and future choices for my life. I knew that this type of living was stifling, but yet I didn't seem to know how to break free.

Then came age 26! Something happened. The light turned on in my brain and all of a sudden I began to question why I did the things I did.

Let me share some questions I had to ask myself, some to which you may be able to relate:

1) What determined my career choice when I was

young? Was it as a result of ensuring that I got the nod of approval from adults in having ambition for an impressive profession? Or was it to ensure that I would earn lots of money when I grew up. I remember seeing my father beaming (or so I thought), and the pride I felt when I told adults that my ambition was to be a lawyer. Not to mention the response I got from these adults. I also remembered the response these adults would give to a child who claimed that his ambition was to "work in an office" or worse if the answer was "I don't know". Now I certainly understand that encouraging a child to reach for the stars is good but responding negatively to a child's innocent response at that age only engendered negative feelings within the child. As a result of these reactions, many children were sucked into the expectation of choosing careers in which they had no real interest or aptitude just to impress others.

2) What affected my choice of a spouse? Was it love, his love for God, his ambition, potential to gain wealth, intelligence, his physical attractiveness? Now I pray that we all be blessed with a husband who is handsome, but let's face it, he could be as ugly as a mug but is the sweetest person who best fits you. People's opinion should not come into play here. Okay, so he is not the hottest guy in the world, he is not in a high paying job, the English Language and he are distant cousins, and he could do well with a little sharpening up in the clothes department, but does that really matter all that much? These are things that can be worked on together. Plus, if you love him and feel that your connection is grounded in God, who cares what others think? It's a pity that many of us choose the wrong partner as a result of a

friend or family's silly advice. It's your life, choose well and live it.

3) What is the worst that could happen if I overturn the applecart? Now I'm not saying go ahead and create chaos in situations, but rather, go ahead and ask the questions that counter popular opinions, open new opportunities for thought and provide new possibilities of solutions. I know that this will initially make you a bit unpopular, but in the end, the wise will see your worth and the ones who will dislike you are not worth worrying over because their envy of you will still cause them to dislike you regardless of your efforts to include them in the process. Leave them to God. The benefit to you is tremendous. Letting your voice be heard is liberating, and the more you do it, the more you will realize that your ideas are not as silly as you had been lead to believe.

4) What if I said no sometimes? I have struggled with this concept for a while and because I was brought up to show good manners, and willingness to "get along" with others, I would most of the times not able to say a direct no when I meant no. I was always concerned about hurting the feelings of others to my own detriment. The ridiculous thing was that I would be immensely angry at myself afterwards when my inability to be direct would cause others to take advantage of me. For me, my sweetness was my weakness and I had to learn to toughen up. Here's the more ridiculous part; it seemed that this inability to speak up was only in effect at certain times, because my many persons will tell you that I am a no-nonsense vocal girl when it comes to matters of injustice or making

presentations that I am passionate about. I realized that my fear to disappoint others was largely a great determining factor of my penchant to always say yes.

I didn't want to be seen as the "bad guy". I have long heard of and usually abided by the adage "It's nice to be nice". Sounds familiar? It is nice to be nice but not when you have sacrificed your priorities and especially not when the individuals that make the requests, seem to be totally oblivious to the effect of their demands on you. Sometimes you have to open your mouth and express what you're feeling. Learn how to say it though. Focus on expressing the way you feel rather than accusing the individual. I have come a far way, but I'm getting there.

5) What is so bad about confrontation? Personally, I am not confrontational. I avoid it like the plague, but in life I have had to deal with a few tricky situations that have taught me that dealing with an issue forthrightly is far better than letting the matter simmer. This is true in all types of relationships. Making time to deal directly with matters that affect the quality of a relationship is crucial for its success. However, uncomfortable, it must be done and many times you may have to be the one to initiate the move towards reconciliation.

6) Can anyone really run me out of town if I follow my own individual style? Okay, so no-one wants to look like the hermit that just crawled out from under a rock when everyone else is rocking the popular fashion. However, whether its clothes, car or any other material item, there comes a point when we must realize that these things are

immaterial to life itself. I'm not encouraging that
we exchange our regular wear with sackcloth, but
following up the latest fashion can be time
consuming and expensive. It forces many to live
above their means. When purchasing a car,
sometimes ignored are the practical reasons like,
good mileage, small engine to save on gas,
availability and affordability of car parts. Don't get
me wrong, having nice things is fine, especially
when you have worked hard to achieve it, I'm
rather suggesting that you should be so strong in
your own convictions that your choices should be
about you and not to impress others. As human
beings afflicted with egos and pride, this may be
challenging, but it is most rewarding to free
yourself from the baggage of living up to other
people's opinion. Life is about living. It is hardly
living when you are abiding in the confines of
people's opinions and objections.

2 Timothy 1:7
"For the Spirit God gave us does not make us timid,
but gives us power, love and self-discipline."

New International Version (NIV)

Use the sound mind that God gave you and live the life
that God intended. He meant for you to fulfill the purpose
He designed for you. Listening to the voices of others
instead of your own voice will thwart your success at
achieving the purpose that is custom-made for you. No
one else can fulfill it but you. Discern the meaning of
words that are spoken over your life and determine who is
for you and who is not. God's voice can be heard directly

as well as through others. Listen for His guidance and allow him to speak to you and eventually through you. Your voice needs to be heard. Determine to be strong enough to make choices irrespective of other people's opinions.

CHAPTER 16
WHAT JUST HAPPENED?

I stared in silence at the walls of my room, wondering, "What next? Having just learnt the day before, that my probationary tenure at my job had come to an unsuccessful end and still filled with mixed emotions, I stared into nothingness. How do I make sense of it? Having been successful several months before in the interviewing process, where the outgoing head executive spoke highly of my skills and qualifications, I now experience a change of guard and suddenly, things go downhill.

My mind quickly raced to my initial thoughts of possibilities as I had applied for the position. A large company, great salary, great position; what more could a girl ask for? Through prayer, I left it in the hands of the Lord to work it out. I also had a friend there who had followed up the process and assisted in moving things along. After about a month or two, I got the call. Three months after that, I was in the position ready to learn. But, things changed. The senior person was now new and, with a new management style, his expectations were different from his predecessor. From day one, I felt uneasy with the new boss and prayed constantly about the situation. Communication was strained between us and as a result, his expectations were, at times, a mystery to me and therefore went unmet. Then it struck me! His job was to look at the bigger picture and that, regardless of my being new to the position and never being in previously similar roles, he had a job to do and he needed to be surrounded by persons already experts at their job. A new mandate from the company's head office was eventually handed down and that paved the way for my departure.

In the exit meeting, I sensed that he was possibly alone in his decision even though the HR manager was present. He spoke succinctly and directly, which I appreciated, not desiring to be in his presence longer than necessary, for I felt , and even shared with a couple friends a few days earlier, that something was about to happen. The meeting only confirmed my premonition.   The HR Manager seemed sincere and empathetic, quite unlike the stoic aura that resonated from the senior manager. I laughed to myself thinking "Lord is this you giving me the desires of my heart?" I had shared with Him many times about my concerns relating to the job and the strained working relationship with the senior executive. I raised myself up, shook hands with the HR Manager and mustered all the strength I could to do the same with my boss. He smiled brightly and said "All the best" seemingly relieved that I hadn't burst into tears or into a fit of rage because God knows I was tempted to do both or either.

"What just happened, Lord?" I asked myself the question as I headed back to my desk. "How grossly unfair!" I had been given a new portfolio to manage with little guidance, judged by a man who never interviewed me but came with his preconceived expectations, not given clearly outlined duties related to the new portfolio, and then given the shaft as part of the company's restructuring exercise. Anger, disappointment, frustration, inadequacy were just some of the feelings that I was experiencing. My friend who had been there from the start had little to say as he was in disbelief regarding the turn of events.

He, my family and close friends had all been supportive

and I truly appreciated every encouraging word I received.

Thinking about it more deeply though, I realized that I learnt a few things in the process.

I even shared these eureka moments with my friends and most of them thought I was being negative, but let me share the lessons that I have learnt.

1) Your present situation is not your final destination. Placing it in context, I refer to the idea that moving on from my previous job was necessary at the time that I did, having spent 13 years there, I felt stagnated and desired personal growth. This new job was to me my next great move where I could settle in comfortably, possibly until retirement, but it was not so. My friends argued, "What was the sense for the Lord to take you from one job to place you in a job only for a limited time?" It made no sense. One day though, it just came to me. I learnt that this was not my final destination and that this move was merely leading me to where I needed to be. God knew that in order for me to get up and move from where I was, I had to be enticed by something apparently better, bigger and sweeter. A great job offering had to be provided in order for me to be tempted to move. This leads me to my second lesson.

2) The door that is opened leads us into greater opportunities for change. The new job I thought was the ultimate reason for moving. Instead it was a channel that lasted only long enough for me to understand that there is far greater in me to accomplish than this. The door that opened was enticing and looked good, and at one point, I had desired to stay. But this was not to be. God led me down the halls of my new home, He led me into different rooms where I

experienced some dining and social pleasures, but I soon found out that I was being led towards the exit door. Clearly, I see now that God never intended for me to stay but He used it as a means to get me out of complacency and get moving.

3) There is a good in everything. My fairly short tenure did bring benefits. Knowledge gained, income earned, exposure to international business standards and the meeting of new friends. Aahh yes, friends, some of whom are still in my life. Many of whom were with me, encouraging me and assisting me in whatever way that they could. A situation is never all positive or all negative. There is always two sides of a coin, two angles to view things and two responses from which to choose. I chose to respond positively.

4) Inadequacy is in the mind. The new job environment was filled with many persons who acted as if they were better than others just from the mere fact that they were working at the company. It was disgustingly funny actually. This culture was very evident in the remarks that would have been made about some of the persons who had left after a short time. "Poor so and so… she couldn't meet the standard, she couldn't keep up or she couldn't cut it so she had to run and leave the work!" I shook my head thinking that they would say the same about me now that I am gone, and I started to feel a bit inadequate. I soon realized that that thought was preposterous! The innate talents and skills that one possesses are not by accident but by design, and I have learnt that not fitting into someone's culture or work style does not mean that an individual has nothing to offer. He still has plenty to offer!

5) Understanding your worth is how God intended for you to live and no man should be allowed to take that

from you. I had to remind myself that my potential lies not in the opinion of others but in the realization that God has equipped me with specific skills that are unique to me. I had to learn also, that these skills may not be the best fit in my present role, but it doesn't make it less valuable. Finding the right fit is key. Many leaders today were square pegs in round holes in many positions they held before they found the right fit. They achieved great success because they found a compatible outlet to utilize their innate skills to produce maximum output.

"So what's the next step?" I am asked almost daily. My answer is clearer now than yesterday. I am getting up and heading out into a new thing that God is even now orchestrating.

CHAPTER 17
FINAL THOUGHTS

The great defender does not promise that He will protect us from every hurt, sadness, or every trouble, but He does promise to work everything out for our good.

Romans 8:28

"And we know that in all things God works for the good of those who love him, who have been called according to his purpose."

New International Version (NIV)

This scripture tells me that all things, good or bad, will work together for good for me because I love God and because I know that I am a part of the called according to HIS purpose.

I thank God that I was able to learn and am still learning from occurrences in my life. I am even more thankful that I was given a desire to share. I hope that as you journeyed with me, page by page, line by line, word by word, you were encouraged and you were able to see things a little bit differently. Whether it is an experience of death, soured relationships, career changes or a major shift in your life, there is always a lesson to be learnt. A deeper lesson than that which meets the eye; one that requires some time alone and a willingness to allow God to open your eyes to more insightful revelation.

For me, I have learnt in marriage that if both of you want it bad enough, it can work, in death, a faithful life secures your eternity in God, in career choices, a shut door will lead you towards other open doors and in making major decisions, little is much when God is in it.

In life there are choices to make and one must be true to oneself and to God in the process. I've also realized that in relationships, no-one is perfect, but finding your best fit is ideal. If, however, you marry a close fit, with God, success can still be yours.

Life is fraught with everyday lessons. It delivers these lessons many times by throwing unexpected curved balls which at times may turn your world upside down. Learning from these experiences is always crucial and many times it will bring about the purpose that you were intended to accomplish. Remember, when life throws you a curved ball, let it bend you towards another direction and then begin again.

"The willow which bends to the tempest, often escapes better than the oak which resists it; and so in great calamities, it sometimes happens that light and frivolous spirits recover their elasticity and presence of mind sooner than those of a loftier character"

Sir Walter Scott

"Notice that the stiffest tree is most easily cracked, while the bamboo or willow survives by bending with the wind."

Bruce Lee

"Be still and know that He is God. For the pathways steep and rough, not what He brings but who He is, will always be enough"

Anonymous

Psalm 46:10

"Be still, and know that I am God."

New International Version (NIV)

ABOUT THE AUTHOR

A writer and mother of two, Dionne-Sheree seeks to instill good values in whomever she associates. A Marketing and Communications specialist by profession, she received her BSc. and M.A. Degrees at the University of the West Indies in Jamaica and achieved the Associate Certified Chartered Marketer designation from the Chartered Institute of Marketing in London after completing a Post Graduate Diploma in Marketing at that institution.

Dionne-Sheree enjoys music of many genres and her inspiration comes from God, family, close friends and nature. Her first book, FLOWER IN YOUR PAIN, was written with the desire to help others understand that their purpose still waits to bloom even after pain has threatened the birth of the flower that lies within. She continues to share her thoughts through several online and other direct channels.

deesheree@yahoo.com and deesheree4@gmail.com
Facebook: DSheree Smith
Facebook: Flower In Your Pain
Twitter: Dee @deesheree2

CPSIA information can be obtained
at www.ICGtesting.com
Printed in the USA
LVOW13s0959190718
584324LV00026B/378/P